Dead or in Prison

By Yahu

The untold stories of at risk youth in New Zealand

Published by WPRR
New Zealand

Text ©Yahu (2015)

Front cover Illustrations © 5th Floor Consultants
http://5thfloorconsultant.blogspot.co.nz/

ISBN 978-0-473-34407-8

Publisher: WPRR
Contact: www.WritersPlotReadersRead.nz
writersplotreadersread@outlook.com
Publication date: 2015

Acknowlegements

To keep this process safe I have had Korero (conversations) with Kaumatua, Kuia and those learned in Reo, to define, articulate and analyse breakdown of Maori words, with consideration of Tikanga.

"I treasure the strands of my cultural cloak. Our songs, music, dances, stories, history, art forms, rituals of welcome and celebration, reinforce my identity, and absolute uniqueness. I celebrate and see each day as perfect, through song and laughter, and just being me"
(Rose Pere, Te Wheke, 1997)

Interweaved into the models are principles and Whakaaro (thoughts) from other recognised Maori theorists including Mason Durie, Hine Wirangi, Hirini Moko Mead.

Also Rose Pere who read my initial work and responded:

"Kia ora koe e Te Rangatira, Nga mihi nui ki I a koe, mo to Kaupapa, It is very important for us to stand in our own power and wisdom. As a traditional Maori, I have a holistic approach to life, but I can also handle the western world's "bits & pieces" knowledge code. Thanks for sharing your paper with me, and I am sure you will Excel, I would like to share a tool of assessment that I and many other people use to assess our total well-being, based on "Te Wheke" a Model of learning/teaching that has been transmitted from our ancient Ancestors.
I wish you well in all your endeavours."
Naku noa,
Na Rangimarie Turuki Rose Pere.

Contents

Introduction

I want to apologize for some of the language in this book, but I need to articulate blatantly and bring context to situations. If I censor this, it won't do this kaupapa justice.

A well-known expert in psychology once told me that when young people swear it is because they can't truly communicate how they feel.

I need you to feel anger, pain, and the voice of these young people's stories, because no one ever gave a shit about them except God.

These times were hard but I believe extreme behaviours require an extreme response.

I want to commit this book to my beautiful partner and our four awesome children who I love and value.

To the families that took me in as an at risk youth, you kept me alive and out of prison.

It was six am. I wanted to be early on my first day of the job. Through the big steel doors, out of nowhere, I saw a foot come flying towards my head! (just missed). I could hear my heart pumping; in front of me stood a young guy and he greeted me with these words:

"You must be a boxer G."

I don't remember the next couple of hours, but I do recall sitting at the table with a group of high risk young people having breakfast. I thought to myself, *why isn't anyone finishing or getting up?*

Then I heard the voice of the nurse...

"Now hand the knife over Sam, and then we can all leave the table."

"I don't have the fucken knife!"

He pulled the knife out of his pants and threw it on the table.

"I don't care; I've got knives hidden all over this unit!"

That day was spent breaking up fights between two young people, one who used homemade push up blocks and another chair. I was not restraint trained at the time, and neither were the other staff. This was my introduction to youth lock up, no training, sink or swim.

Chapter one: "Bart"

When I first met Bart I hadn't been in youth work long. It was his first day in lock up.

The reason I noticed him was that he isolated himself away from the other children.

Bart was underweight (like many that were admitted). I asked if he would like to play chess. He didn't say much, but I noticed that he laughed to himself a lot for no apparent reason.

Every movement in a lock up is planned. It's like a prison but a bit more relaxed. I have discovered since that they are currently looking at "therapeutic ways of practice" with a focus on restraint minimization, and less time in isolation or secure care units.

How this is going, I am unsure. But back then it was different.

If young people didn't listen, they were placed in "time out", reviewed every twenty minutes, then "time out two" and so on. If they became a threat to themselves or others, they were placed in "secure care" which is basically a concrete cell exactly like a jail cell.

I know what you are thinking: eleven to fourteen year olds in New Zealand, locked in concrete cells without a mattress between the hours of seven am and seven pm? Yes, it's true.

I have supported some of New Zealand's most violent, disturbed, and hurt young people. I have spent weeks in secure care units with Rangatahi.

This was the beginning of my learning journey into mental illness and what it feels like to be locked up.

That night he was placed in secure care because he pulled the middle finger to a worker.

He was reviewed at twenty-four hours; his time was extended to three days then five, due to violent outbursts towards staff, throwing food, tables, shit, and piss - pretty much anything he could.

This is where I came in. I worked with Bart nearly every day for three months.

Bart was highly unpredictable; he would screw up little pieces of paper and put them into door locks, jamming them, and he would try to damage his cell, punch staff, or scratch them with his long nails (it hurts!)

One night he shoved a whole blanket and all his clothes down a toilet.

I saw him once stab a guy with a pen, just missing the eye. For a while there, he needed to be restrained once an hour.

When it came to behaviour, Bart was the king of chaos.

As his mental state began to worsen, he started to hear voices, and then voice commands telling him what to do. Bart even ate his own shit. A friend of mine told me that when patients start to play with or eat their own shit, it is a sign of madness.

Then he began to get scared of the voices.
Bart would ask me to do karakia (prayers) for him. We also sang songs together. Bart went from unit to unit, then jail, and finally forensic wards.

I supported him for a total of two and a half years. It was because of him I wanted to learn more about mental health.

I learnt that Bart didn't have a correct assessment; he had been misdiagnosed. He had foetal alcohol syndrome and then schizophrenia.

One day I was sitting with Bart in the open unit. I taught him there because no teacher at the on-site School could handle his erratic traits. Bart had the mental age of probably a ten year old.

I asked him to draw me a picture. He drew a stick figure and another one holding what looked like a hammer. I asked:

"What is that?"

He responded:

"This is me when I got locked in cupboards and hit in the head with a hammer."

This is the reality for some young people in New Zealand right now: exposed to violence, torture, and neglect.

If Bart had actually been diagnosed correctly, maybe the right supports could have been put in place to delay his journey to prison.

I firmly believe that being contained in cells for long periods of time was a contributing factor to his rapid decline in mental state.

I want to make it clear that I never sent him to lock up, ever.

I just looked after him because no one else wanted to.

This was actually what kept me employed during that time - my high tolerance of working with the "disturbed" and violent young people.

I could relate to them on many levels. I have experienced isolation, rejection, and being away from my family.

Chapter two: "Lisa"

I met Lisa on my first week working in the community. This type of work was all new. Youth lock up had been predictable, a routine; when something happened, you knew what the outcome or response was, whilst in the community each day was different and quite unsafe.

Lisa's file had been given to me from another youth worker who had told me that she was fine and could be discharged.

But I wanted to make sure. At the house, as I walked up the long drive way, I could smell two things: weed and spray paint.

As I got to the entrance, Lisa ushered me in and she said:

"Quick, look at this!"

I walked up to the bathroom, opened the door, and there stood a guy approximately fourteen years of age.

His face was covered in spray paint and he smelt of dope. He was rocking backwards and forwards, yelling:

"Uuuuuh! aaaaw!"

Out of his mind on solvents. I thought, *shit, what am I to do?*

I left the property and rang youth aid and the police. As I waited outside, I noticed a third young person - let's call him Larry - and I said to him:

"Who gave that guy the weed?"

He replied:

"Ummm, me..."

"And who gave her the spray paint?"

"Oh, me..."

I said to Larry:

"That's ok if you want to do drugs, that's your deal, but once you give it to someone else, what if they end up dead?"

Ok, let's stop for a second. I've told this story to many people and I've asked this question:

"Where are Lisa, Larry, and the guy high on spray paint now?"

I usually get an array of answers. But here is the truth.

Years later, Larry died from a butane overdose. He fell off a bridge and broke his neck.

The young man that was wasted died after sniffing three cans of fly spray. It was reported as death from natural causes.

Where is Lisa? Alive. She has a job and a child. She got the support she needed. This is a big part of why she is still alive today.

Sure, she left school at a young age, didn't get NCEA level one, smoked a lot of her step father's dope, and developed a drug induced psychosis for a time, but she became an amazing artist and painter.

Her success lay in two things. She had someone that supported her, and she found what her strength was. Art. I've seen her family portraits she drew. Amazing.

A side note about other drugs

I once supported a "meth cook"; she was only fourteen and making five thousand dollars a week for a gang. She could hardly read and write but she knew the big long names of chemicals. Sad. She was exploited by this gang. Her mother was also in jail for murder.

Any one that uses kids to cook drugs is scum. Stay away from meth. Get help.

I have seen grown men cry and beg gangs not to murder their family because of meth debt, or what is called "ticking". I have visited hundreds in mental health wards that are "drug fucked".

Synthetics

The product founder or guru's good friend died from the party drug rinse.
I believe that was the motivation in the beginning of the formulation of "safe alternative drugs". It was a genuine search, but quickly escalated into something so destructive.

How much could a synthetic shop make?

Between seventy and eighty thousand dollars a week.
The problem was tax.

They would declare their income as seven thousand a week. Tax evasion is why our government temporarily shut down the shops, not the drug problems of the people.

Straight profit

These synthetic labs cost approximately one million each to set up. It's probably cheaper to cook meth.

I saw mothers, fathers, and grandparents of all cultures buying synthetics. Those drugs didn't discriminate.

The average age for drug and alcohol use for young people over the years has lowered, with kids trying weed, alcohol, and cigarettes around nine years old, or in their first year of intermediate.

I'm actually more shocked when I meet a young person who hasn't tried drugs by sixteen.

I saw the boxes of packets imported in from Asia; they cost about a dollar wholesale with a mark-up of thirty to forty dollars a pack.

One day, at a youth group I was running, a small girl came up to me and said:

"Mummy cut daddy last night, with a knife."

From further questioning, I realised that mummy and daddy had been spotting weed on the stove, and mummy had passed out and cut daddy by accident. Other incidents included a guy bringing a petrol bomb to church, and many other things.

Chapter three: "Milhouse"

I was first called to his place a few years back.

He was experiencing visions and seeing things that no one else could see. These were beginning to bother him.

His father didn't want him to see a doctor because they had other members of their family that had been through the mental health system. I respected their wishes and left.

A week later I was notified that Milhouse had to appear in youth court for assault.

When I got there I requested of the police that a mental state assessment be done, but they refused. By law, the police can hold a person for seventy-two hours until a mental health clinician comes.

I have noticed in recent times that, due to high numbers of youth in crisis, various mental health teams are unable to put adequate supports in place for them.

It was Friday afternoon and here we were, outside the courthouse. Milhouse had no shoes, he was mentally unwell, and he could not return to the address because of the assault. Great one.

Then it dawned on me: Whanau Connections. I managed to find a cousin to hold Milhouse for the weekend.

On Monday I took him to the mental health team at the hospital to remain in their care (or so I thought). He was delusional, believing that he was a martial artist, speaking gibberish, and trying to do martial arts on the nurses and patients.

Later in the week I went to visit him at the ward. I walked up to the counter:

"Where is Milhouse?"

The fact is that no one knew where he was, not the doctors or the nurses. I found him on the roof of the carpark building! And he was out of his mind on synthetics.

When synthetic cannabis had just come out in New Zealand, at its worst I saw up to fifteen students a day at a high school under the influence of those truly evil drugs.

So where is he today?

He committed suicide in one of the units, coming off synthetics and weed.

At the time, this was only the second young person I had known to commit suicide.
Since then I have worked with at least one hundred that have had suicidal thoughts, or attempted to die through self harm.

I have taught harm minimization strategies to

advocate for youth suicide attempts to be taken more seriously, as it is my world view that currently it isn't being treated seriously enough by clinical teams.

Stop thief

There are a lot of one-liners out there, like:

"Treat them good because one day you will meet them on the outside."

(Or they might move in next door).

One day, as I backed out of my drive way, I saw one of the meanest thieves from the lock up standing right outside my house. I thought to myself, *should I hide?*

I jumped out and warmly shook their hand.

"How are you doing?"

Ok, they replied.

A few weeks later I learnt that they had been on the run at the time; they had robbed fifteen houses and a warehouse, but didn't steal from me.
I believe that this was about respect. I had treated them well so they returned the favour. (Or maybe there was just nothing worth stealing).

This isn't always the case.

There are many I have helped, but they turned on me the first chance they got.

But I can look back and be confident that I fought for Whanau, Hapu, and Iwi. It does sadden me sometimes that the feeling or respect wasn't mutual.

So what is it that young people want?

It could be food, money, or your time.

I was in a lecture on child development once and they were discussing the teenage brain as a computer that is offline trying to reformat. They stated a young person will come back online if there is mention of food or money.

I have tried this in group programmes at schools and you would be amazed at how true this is. But most of all, they want time; they spend eight hours with their friends a day (not counting Facebook) and an average of twenty minutes with their parent/s or family.

You wonder who they will listen to and be influenced by more.

Chapter four: "Nelson"

Nelson came from a big family. Exposed to fourteen years of domestic violence, he watched his mother being bashed and controlled by his father.

The anger within him grew over the years, until one day he tried to kill himself.

I wasn't there when this happened. It was reported that it was an attempted hanging. In front of people.

I was called to the hospital. I stayed with him for six hours, making sure he didn't leave. The clinical team finally saw him; they didn't appear to know where to put Nelson because he was young.

So I came up with a plan. I would take him to a community safe house and stay with him all night until the next morning, then take him to see the child adolescent team.

The doctors agreed. That was a long two days. I had been working from that morning until the five o'clock admission; I stayed up all night and worked until five the next day, twenty-four hours.

The child team assessed Nelson's risk as "low", even though three weeks later Nelson became mentally unwell, due to not taking his medication, and attempted to assault family members.

The mental health team said his risk was "low". It took a lot of police officers to restrain him.

When released, Nelson went back to his mother's with no risk plan and he continued to assault. Nothing was done by the five services involved. Except for us.

Suicide

In the last three months, attempted suicide by young people has increased by fifty percent in the Wellington region. The women's refuge reports that nine out of ten males threaten to kill themselves, but they don't know why these figures have increased dramatically.

When young people say they want to end their life, they need to be heard. Not ignored. A picture has been painted that suicide is down. This is incorrect. Successful attempts are down. But suicidal thoughts and attempts are rapidly increasing.

This could be due to an increase in "social stressors" such as debt, relationship breakdown, and other what I call "combos" of events which a person can no longer tolerate.

Life is seen by some as a burning building; sooner or later it gets too hard to stay inside, and they decide to jump out of a window.

I have been called to and talked many young people out of killing themselves. It is common for them to hear voices or thoughts telling them to die, and you would actually be surprised by how common that is.

My belief is that suicide is and should be talked about; it might just keep a person alive.

People have been shocked by my approach. I just ask them:

"Have you ever self harmed? Thought about dying? Attempted to die? What did you use? How did you feel when you woke up still alive?"

The only people that seem to not want to talk about suicide are social services.

Taxi driver therapy

One of the most effective ways of getting a young person to talk is driving somewhere. You know when you jump in a taxi and "nek minnut" sharing the whole life story to a total stranger?

I call my work car my "office" for that reason.

Funerals

Over recent times I have attended a lot of funerals. The most powerful was a Tangi full of gang members and their children.

They wore and laid colours on the coffin. Their colours were no longer about the gang. It was more than that, the connection to the death.

I have seen young dead people with their sounds playing off their phone next to the coffin.

I have sat listening to young people cry. In one case, I listened to a girl that was meant to be in the car that crashed, but wasn't.

A chance to live.

So what is self harm?

To different people it means different things; in older times, culturally, it was a sign of grief, the loss of a loved one. But to this generation it is an outward sign of an internal pain.

I have listened openly to over one hundred young male, female, and transgender who have and still do self harm. Some cut their arms, legs, even faces with glass, blades, and wire from pens. I believe it is important to listen.

Hear what is it they are worried or depressed about. Just because they self harm that doesn't mean they want to die, but there is definitely a link between suicide and self harm.

I see drug and alcohol use as self harm, and putting oneself in unsafe situations as self harm.

It is easy to be distracted by the behaviour but one needs to keep this separate from the young person.

See the behaviour as a "symptom of the sickness".

What is the reason for the behaviour?

Chapter five: "Ralf"

Ralf was one of the most violent young people I have worked with. I don't know what happened to him, but I'm sure he must be in jail.

An extensive criminal history, Ralf would steal at least three cars a week and sell them to gangs for about one thousand dollars a car.

One day in the secure lock up unit (in which he spent three months) Ralf was sitting at the table boasting as usual about his crimes. He turned to me and said:

"I make more money in a day than what you earn in a week!"

To which I responded:

"That is true, but you are getting ripped off. They sell those cars for thirty thousand each and you only make a grand a car, and while the gang is free, counting their money, you are sitting in here, locked up."

While I went on my break, it was reported that Ralf had become unsettled and had to be locked in his cell. When I returned I could hear a banging noise and then the sound of breaking glass, the sound of piping being tampered with and a *whoosh!*

We decided to ring the police as water came running from under the cell door.

The officer arrived with pepper spray, *"ready"*. We opened the cell door; it was like a scene out of a Hollywood movie.

Ralf had used a door stop with a metal screw to dig out the ceiling and rip out the pipes, which flooded the cell and smashed the viewing window.

He caused thirty thousand dollars' worth of damage to these so-called indestructible cells.

The day that Ralf left the unit, he was nice to everyone. Except me. He whispered in my ear:

"One day I'm going to find where you live and slit your throat, mother fucker."

The week he was released, he jumped on a plane and reportedly head-butted an air hostess, breaking her nose.

There are some evil people in this world. Believe me. I have met them.

Sadly no amount of rehab can change them. I met a guy that cut up his best friend into pieces.

I heard of another who cut a baby in half with a knife while it was still alive.

When I worked in hospital with some murderers, I always remember these words from one inmate:

"You work with those kids aye. You go back and tell them, don't make the same mistakes I did."

There is definitely a link between crime and education. For example, in Wainuiomata and Upper Hutt, there is a high level of youth crime between the hours of twelve midday and four in the afternoon.

One must assume that they are not in school. Education has become my focus as of late, and I have piloted an intervention strategy to retain youth in some form of education.

If youth follow the pathway to youth lock up and prison, their education will be the school of crime.

This school is extremely interesting and appealing. I have seen rope made out of toilet paper, knives from tooth brushes. I have learnt how to destroy five thousand dollar locks, break out of "secure facilities", code languages, tattoo with blades and Indian ink, and how to hide weapons and contrabands in "stashing spots".

Make no mistake. If you allow phones in prison, be prepared for your phone number, address, and family members to be sourced by inmates.

You should understand that criminal thought and patterns of offending are always an option when you have to provide for a young family.
I empathize with dealers, because they are trying to make money just like everyone else.

The three levels to legit

There are some who live on a pure income from crime, others who earn a "semi legit" and "not so legit" lifestyle.

All the families I have supported, I have encouraged the full transition to living a legal lifestyle, being drug or alcohol free, and not having to hide every time you hear the police.

Chapter six: "Todd"

He was only five when I met him, the youngest offender I have met. He smoked cigarettes, climbed power poles, stole, had no fear.

There were concerns that his mother may have used drugs or alcohol when he was in the womb. Highly unpredictable and compulsive, he was kicked out of two primary schools, often found on the roofs of houses.

I did have one positive outcome; I got funding to take him to rock climbing. He could scale the highest walls there. A group of army cadets were present; they were amazed at his talent to climb.

"Homer"

Once I met this guy who knew how to damage property, in every house he was placed in, and smashed windows. No one could handle him.

He used to like breaking into glue factories or sitting with mates, high on petrol. His friends told me that one day he even thought the can was a real person.

Every night when I was on a shift he would ask:

"Can I talk to you?" or *"Can I come live at your house?"*

"Bob"

One of the first transgender kids I met, Bob, was an amazing singer, and he loved wearing women's clothing. Raised by drag queens, he knew nothing else. The saddest sight was when I was called to his room one night, where he had cut up all his arms and wrists with broken glass.

I believe as a social worker, there are situations one must come to accept.

Firstly, people make their own choices. Kids die.

I remember going to a support meeting for a young gang member on the Friday. The cop said to him:

"Now don't steal any more cars."

I shook his hand and said:

"We'll catch up, I'll see you next week."

"Yeh bro."

I saw him next week. In a coffin.

He had stolen a car and killed two of his friends after robbing a petrol station.
Everyone was wearing blue, throwing colours on the coffin.

The story goes that after the Tangi, they took the coffin back to the house, pulled the body back out, and smoked weed and drunk for weeks.

The kids actually looked after the babies while the adults smoked synthetics and weed, and drunk until they got evicted.

Secondly, don't change the world; some people are happy where they are.

They love drugs and crime; nothing you can say or do will change their minds, unless they want to.

A few years ago I coined the phrase "functionalised dysfunctionalism", which refers to families that behave in such a chaotic way - beating the crap out of each other, drugging, and drinking - but who still stay together.

Usually these are the ones who know how to work the system, "play the game", say what you want to hear.

My advice: leave them to it. There's nothing you can do.

Thirdly, look after yourself.
Don't be a cowboy like me in my first few years, just rocking up to gang or drug houses by myself.

Check for dogs

I've had a few close calls. An example is when I went to a known drug courier's house to find a kid, a third generation gang member.

I walked into the house. There were at least ten

kids on some type of drug. I got a bad feeling. I shook the kid's hand, said something like *"catch you later"*, and left.

I drove home, turned on the television to the news, and I got the shock of my life. Fifty cops raiding the house I had just been at.

They found people hiding in the roof of the place with weapons!

"Knives and machetes."

Speaking of weapons, when you attend a house visit, try to have someone with you if you can. Check for exits, cameras and hazards, and always have a charged phone on you.

Once I went to this house, because this guy had been wagging school. I thought we got along ok.

I was wrong. That day as I was leaving, he tried to jump me with a knife; I managed to restrain him and ring the police.

Also on another occasion, a guy threatened me with a machete. I managed to negotiate my way out of that one but yep, be careful out there.

He said:

"The pigs come, I don't care! I'll cut them too!!"

Be prepared to be sworn at, gossiped about, assaulted, spat on (or your food), chased by dogs, have your privacy breached, receive complaints, ignored, have care plans sabotaged, questioned, have your life threatened, stalked, have doors slammed, have hits put on you, have your property and car damaged, and be scratched and bitten. But worst of all, my favourite: scabies and head lice.

At one property, there was a kitchen with grease like candle wax, dust everywhere like actual snow, a bathroom rubbed in faeces, and – wait for it – a bucket of shit in the middle of the lounge.

A team of us went in there to clean. During which my mate was chucking me down items out the window to put in the skip bin.

As we finished, I watched as people started to emerge from their houses to salvage "items of value" that had been thrown out.

Know your role, your strengths and weakness.

If you aren't a counsellor, don't pretend to be one. It's not about you. It's about the young people and their family determining their future pathway, not you telling them.

Things a social worker cannot accept or ignore: neglect, kids with no food (breakfast, lunch, or tea) and kids that have not bathed and smell bad.

Domestic violence

It's funny this one; because I have stopped so many violent incidences in the community, some have associated me with violence.

I have gotten between couples, stopped people from stabbing, punching, strangling, and even a guy walking into a house with a brick. I am restraint trained. And yes, there is a time when you may have to use reasonable force to stop a person harming themselves or others.

Family violence is ugly. I saw a sister of mine dragged by her hair by her mum and dad, punching back and forth like a rag doll, *Bang! Bang!*

Young people are hesitant to "nark" out their parents as they fear they will get a worse hiding.

Sometimes kids need to be uplifted. Sometimes the best place for them is away from their families.

For me this was true.

The best thing I ever did was to get away from my family.

To this day, they are the most dysfunctional family I have ever met.

Hope

Look at the untapped potential of a young person.

Find their strengths, what they enjoy, what they are good at. Art, music, dance, rock climbing, sport.

Once they discover this, you can use these natural talents to formulate goals. If they don't have any, their goal could be to find some.

Deep down, one must not lose sight of the light in the darkness. This hope has kept me for years.

I knew my purpose or "calling" from a young age. I knew I wanted to help people. But at the time I didn't know how. It took a few teachers that showed a step to the right door.

I've known four presidents for the mob who left and became drug and alcohol free, I've known black power members who are far better social workers than others, and I've met a guy who gave up smoking weed whilst living in a tinny house.

I've seen the mongrel mob implement some great rehab intervention against meth in New Zealand. These people give me hope. A famous advocate against family violence once said:

"Only shitheads can help shitheads."

Once a community nurse called me to her office. She then proceeded to grill me in why I was trying to help young people.

She said I should give up, and went on to share that she had a nervous breakdown and had just returned to work.

None of her negative discussion could persuade me to give up the fight for social justice.
A month later I learnt that she had died. That is the point.

Stand up and live. Lie down and die.

Chapter seven: "Twenty Dollar Food Budget"

I have had involvement in prison reintegration. One lady who was a high level offender was left (after rent and power) with fifteen to twenty dollars a week for food.

I would pick her up and off to Pak'nSave: three dollar noodles, four loaves of five dollar bread, four dollar dented cans of baked beans, a nasty tasting packet of coffee for a dollar seventy, four dollar milk, and maybe if we were lucky, a cheap pack of sausages.

When she got out of prison, the police conducted a home visit with a:

"You will be back inside within a month. Welcome to the neighbourhood!"

She stayed out for over a year because I sourced free rubbish bags of bread, and she was under pressure from WINZ to "find a job" or jump on a course.

Imagine the travel costs and humiliation of telling future employers, every week, your offending history.

Medication and doctor's bills

The truth is, there was no rehab, or transition from

prison. Straight private rent.

No money for doctor's visits. No real money for food.

This is the disgusting fact. No one can truly live on a benefit.

Could it be a system designed to fail? To keep us unwell?

I would be laughing if this wasn't so serious. Budget courses, with twenty dollars for food? Did I forget bank fees (once a month)?

Then your food budget is "zero" so how do you budget that? All I can say is she's lucky she didn't have children, take drugs or alcohol, or smoke.

One day I went as usual to check the house when inside I noticed a whole shopping bag of pills. When I asked what it was for, this was the response:

"Oh I got them for free from a mate, in case I get sick. These are for my ADHD."

I said:

"You realize it says here DO NOT combine with any ADHD medication!"

"Oh..."

My point is that it is common for people to hold

medication or borrow others that aren't their own to use, because they can't afford the doctor.

Turning up to the emergency department is a cheaper option.

Children of gang members

I am impressed by what has been happening as of late with the "old dogs" or old leaders of the mongrel mob and black power. They are going back to school, training, and starting to encourage their children to "not be like them". This is not easy though, because for many they want to continue the legacy of gang life.

I have supported many young people whose parents have done long lags (time in jail) or were removed from their parents care. All they knew was crime, violence, and drugs.

How do we teach "common sense"? Well for you, the reader, it could be worlds away from others.

Shoplifting could be a logical solution to hunger, fighting a solution to disputes, running away from home a way to keep safe from dad beating the shit out of mum, walking the gutters for cigarette butts a way to get smokes, carrying a knife a way to protect yourself.

There is a growing trend I have seen, where young people no longer attend school. No rules, no boundaries, unable to cope with what I call "the basics". Many who can't sit in a class for even half an hour without getting into a fight or getting kicked out.

Whether it's social phobia, or post-traumatic stress, or simply hunger. "Feed the kids" is a positive move forward.

Culture and values

In the time of writing this book I have been searching for the final subject matter to contemplate, and today it came. Once a week I attend karakia and waiata sessions at a local Marae.

The kaiako combine with kohanga and teenagers where they sing, recite their whakapapa, and laugh.

I worry in this dark time that these things could be lost. I reflect on the five thousand young people in lock up in New Zealand, disconnected from community, education and whanau, hapu and iwi.

In the last six years, I have watched at least fifteen kaupapa Maori mental health services close, and others come into the firing line as the government sets to discard what they see as "non-essential services".

I have been a part of effective kaupapa Maori social services.
I believe that Whanau Ora is not a funding stream like the government would have us believe; it is an

ancient Te Ao Maori world view of interconnectedness, acknowledging that there can be no separation of the walls of wellness.

As a social worker, I recommend supporting the individual and their connection to whanau, education, health, and community.

A great question was asked this week on the review of a certain department that protects young people: why are no representatives of hapu, iwi, or the Pacific a part of this?

Culture of disentitlement

When I worked in care and protection many years ago, we would see young people come in and out four or more times, and have frequent placement breakdown. This drove me to community work, as I felt I could be more effective in interventions to stop or delay young people from getting locked up.

They call it care and protection. I call it lock up.

You could put a sign on a toilet and call it a dining room.

But the fact remains; it's still a shit house.

Bored of education? So are we

Teaching methods need to change. A counsellor said to me:

"This child is not cut out for mainstream education!"

To which I responded:

"I understand this, but what if forty five percent of your school students coming to your classes present these behaviours?"

The teachers will have to adapt, and learn how to support these children.

The journey to prison

I don't believe that young people choose to go to prison; it is the end result of bad decisions. I have met youth that steal, lie, wag school, assault, run away, do drugs, drink, tag, set fires, and prospect for gangs.

Or they break into houses and cars without giving it a second thought. To them, violence as a response to crisis is so normal and their solution: fight, flight, or freeze. In prison programmes, we unpack the "whakapapa" of offending. Often these patterns started in childhood and it takes years to change.

Often people have the misconception that when a youth is referred to a social service, within weeks they will "change". I call this the "car wash". Actually it takes people a lifetime to make changes.

Firstly, they need to see that what they are doing isn't helping. Sitting in a police cell can bring this realisation, but if not, then a lag in prison away from a girlfriend can.

Prison sucks. You can't smoke there. They give new inmates condoms.

Violence, ugly food, being told where to go and what to do.

Depression, mental illness, disconnection from people.
I try to let youth know what prison will be like.

Some listen but many don't; a few young people I've worked with are just finishing or starting sentences now as I write this.

Many of the founding gang members in New Zealand started in borstals or youth lock ups first before going to jail.

I once stood in an alternative school in Petone with a former gang leader; on the wall of the gym were the names of students. As we stared at the names he muttered:

"Yep knew that one, dead, dead, did a lag with them, jail, jail, dead, stabbed, jail, jail…."

Once I was assisting with a group programme in prison. The men were getting restless, as it had been a long session. There were a variety of offending charges: meth manufacturing to dope growing to beating the shit out of the missus.

I wanted to get their attention and bring the focus back to the kaupapa (agenda), so I grabbed a pen and wrote on the white board:

“The bitch deserved it!!”

One of the older men, who had done numerous ten year lags said:

“That's fucked up man!”

One of the younger nineteen year old guys responded:

“Yeh, yes she did!!”

I waited until they had all finished and then I said:

“What I just did was an assessment, to see your victim empathy. Some of you are sorry for the offending you have committed, for others it will take a couple of lags to realise.”

I was blessed that, as a young offender on the pathway to prison, I had early interventions that helped me see the need to change my thoughts and feelings, which influenced my behaviour.

For many young people, they are being guided by their peers. They have parents who do not give a shit about where they are or what they do.

I meet kids who have not seen their parents in years. Their mates get them to do “keg runs” (running into a supermarket and running out with alcohol). Their friends are not even real, just using each other.

No wonder they don't trust anyone.

Chapter eight: "Models of Practice"

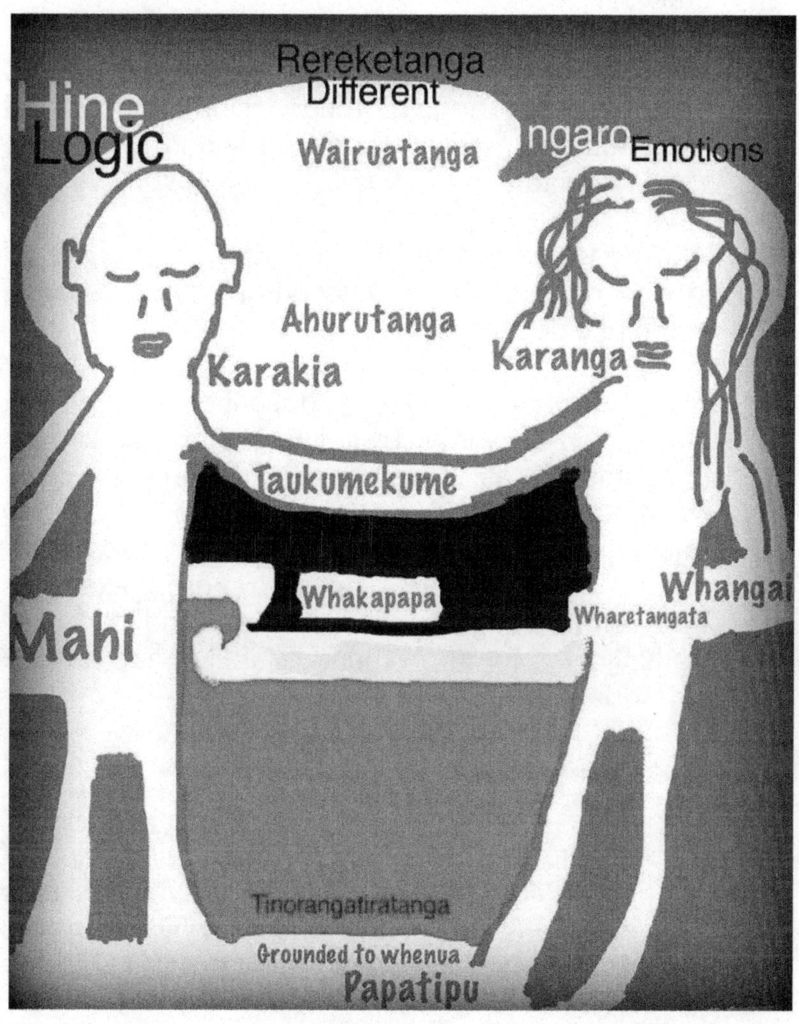

Over my time of study at Te Wananga O Aotearoa, I developed three therapeutic frameworks of practice.

The "Mana Mauri treatment assessment tool", Kaitiake o te Tangata" (supervision model), and "Rereketanga", which will be explained in detail in the next chapter.

Why do we need frameworks? These can guide us in working in complex situations to quickly assess and make decisions.

The Rereketanga model is described through the breakdown of words. I will interpret my Whakaaro (thoughts), as well as feedback from Kaumatua/kuia (elders). Kupu (words) from Iwi (tribes) have smaller words that gave descriptions into the bigger ones. For example: Whakawhanaungatanga, you can find "Whaka" (reduplicated forms), Whanau (family), and au (the individual).

Whanaungatanga:

> *"Captures the all-embracing relationships of pre-1840 Māori society, Māori relationships were between people and the physical world, Atua (spiritual entities)."*
> (NZ Law Commission, 2003)

I believe that respectful relationships are a crucial part of social work in the applied practice. When you have this, it offers people nous of belonging, developed as a result of kinship human rights and obligations.

This is my quest to define the Rereketanga model. **Rereketanga** means different, **RERE:** to flow free, go into an action, gliding movement, **RE:** unseen, unheard. **TA:** colour, DNA, **NGA:** Snarling, growling, gritting of teeth. Everyone is unique in their genetic make-up, colour, and shape.

What others can see and what they can't see in the unseen, the "between" the difference.

There must be tension in difference (Taukumekume). It could be figuring out how to treat others and where to place this tension.

Hinengaro: thoughts, thinking, **HI:** grasp, acquire, something, **NE:** coding to DNA imprints.

Hine: "logic" (Hinewirangi Kohu Morgan personal communications, 2014).

Hine-nui-te-po ("Great woman of night") is a goddess of darkness and death, and the ruler of the underworld in Māori stories. She went to the underworld because she discovered that Tane, whom she had married, was also her father.

The red colour of sunset comes from her. Hine ahuone is acknowledged in Karakia when working with Harakeke. She changed her name to Hine-nui-te-po (from Hine-titama, the daughter of Tane). Sometimes logical thinking can be a painful process; as the saying goes "the truth hurts", or to be Tika and Pono to one's self and others.

A constant internal and external debate between logical and emotional lenses, informed by world views, informed by lived experience and principles, there is argument around what Hinengaro means.

But I believe our thoughts define our actions, therefore we should as practitioners seek to find a balance. If we function in logic, we could limit and place constraints on ourselves or others, but too much on emotion and we may not think clearly in a crisis situation which requires action.

Here is a Karakia recited over Hine-titama by Tane:

> *"Ka Tupu, Ka toru, Ka Whakaiho*
> *Tangata. Toro Te Akaaka, Toro*
> *Te Iho Nui, Toro Te Iho Roa, ka*
> *Whakaupoko, ka*
> *whakaringaringa. Ka*
> *Whakawaewae, ka Whaka tinana*
> *Mai Koe"*

> *"It grows, it extends, a human form*
> *emerges the limb extends, and the big*
> *heart, the long heart develops, the head*
> *develops, the hands the legs and your*
> *body is formed."*
> (Best, 1929)

NGA: many or to take a breath, RO: internal, inside, Ngaro: emotions. Description: to find the balance, to not be too emotional, or too logical to balance the two, and to be sensitive to the space in between, the Mauri (life force) of the person or be present in Wairua.

The first breath was into Hine-titama, TE HEI MAURI ORA. HA, Taonga Tuku Iho (breath, treasures that have come down).

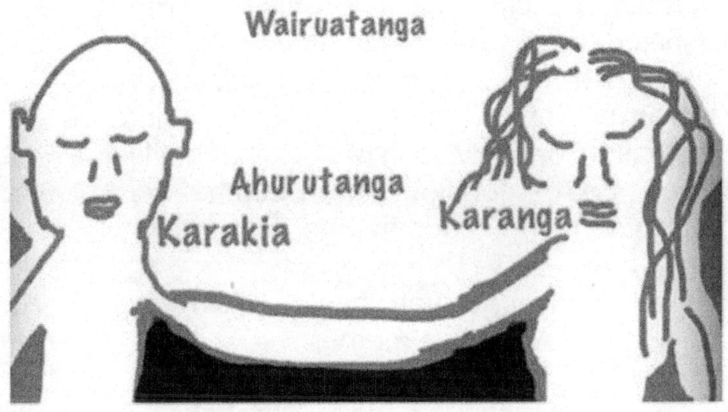

Wairuatanga: spiritual realm, When Wairua is present we are in a state of wellness, **WA** is described as timeless motions. **I:** divine child, cells/things that are in cells, **WAI:** water, **RUA:** two, **TA:** colour DNA, **Nga:** many. A person's Wairua is unique; each treatment needs to be.

So what is **AIO Wairua**?

> *"In a spiritual sense, accountable to the community they served in a temporal sense, aiming at perfection."*
> (Pere, 1997)

Kaitiaketanga (guardianship) is what keeps us and people we support safe (Pohatu, 2010).

AIO: A is the female mother, **I** the divine child, and **O** the male sound or energy. So treatment of people as a Whanau is important; the divine parents, the creator of the universe. Principles of applied practice that can keep and create safe space (**Ahurutanga**) and be a Kaitiake.
Karanga: an exchange of calls, there is no restriction on how long the exchange lasts. First voice, **KA:** fortified to become one, **RA:** enlightenment to become one, **Nga**: many.

Karakia: respite ritual chants, **KARA:** colour, **KI:** energy full, **A:** female mother.

KA means to ignite or spark, **Whakakaa**, TO ignite or spark (Wiremu Wehi, 2014) karakia, and incarnations to the **ATUA**. (Parker, 30/9/14).

Wharetangata: womb, **Wha:** four corners of transformation, **RE:** unseen, unheard, **Tangata:** people, men, persons, human beings, **Whangai:** to feed, nourish, bring up, foster, adopt, raise, nurture, rear.

AROHA: a creative force that comes from the spirit. Seeking unity and balance, **A:** forms and shapes a mental foundation. Female mother, Root word **ARO** meaning mind, seat of feelings, and **HA** meaning breath.

"**ARO** a direction or focus in a specific area" (Parker, 30/9/14).

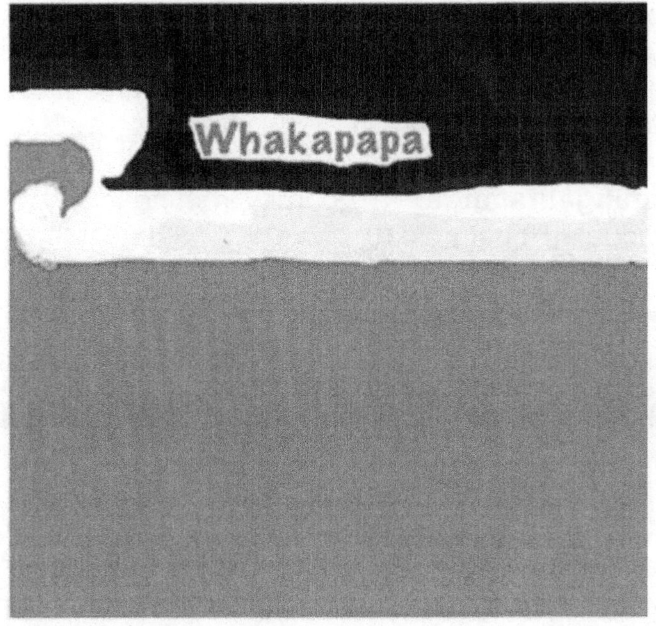

Whakapapa: genealogy lay flat upon each other, lineage, everlasting link, **KA:** to become equal, **Whaka:** to cause something to happen, reduplicated forms,
PA: things you are feeling/see in your heart, good and bad, **PAPA:** father, uncle, dad, **Pepeha:** breath of the Pepe (baby), **HA:** breath, **Kaakano:** seed.

"Most relationships were based on whakapapa (genealogy). Whakapapa was also the basis for social constructions, that being Whanau, Hapū and Iwi."
(NZ Law Commission, 2003)

Papakāinga is a connection to Whenua (land) through the burying of the umbilical cord; 'Papakāinga' refers to **'papa'** or Papatuanuku as the ancestral earth mother and **'kainga'** ancestral home, (Papatipu) a physical environment to sustain your human reality.

Tinorangatiratanga: a journey defined by an individual. (Pohatu, 2010).

So as social workers in New Zealand, how do we find balance between "logical thinking" and empathy? Is it about manipulating a situation or is it about what the whanau wants? What if the whanau is in an unsafe situation but don't realize it?

What about legislation, best practice guidelines, what our organization says in policy? Is it in our mahi we are in constant negotiation to find balance? The Rereketanga model acknowledges that each situation is unique and therefore needs to be assessed case by case.

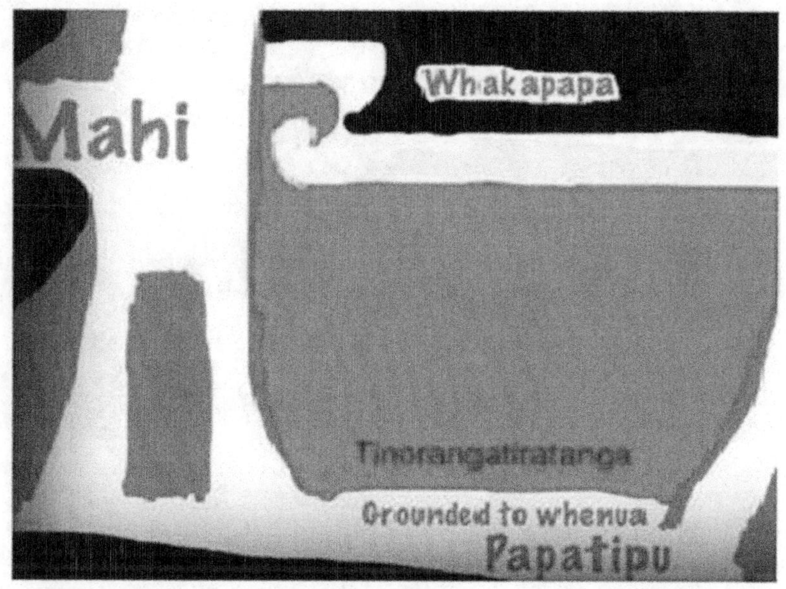

Mahi: to work, make happen, practice, raise, **MA:** understanding, pure, **HI:** grasp or acquire something. Our support should be about Tinorangatiratanga, for the people we work with. **TI:** when balance begins or starts, **NO:** beginning, start, **RA:** enlightenment, can see, **NGA:** many or to take a breath, **TIRA:** travel in a party of travellers, **TANGA:** company.

Ahurutanga: the safe space in between, create or facilitate safe space, through negotiation.

Applied practice (the negotiation to find balance).

A: forms and shapes a mental foundation. Female mother, **HU:** glide, endless movement, infinite, **RU:** synergy working together, energies coming together to create energy, **TANGA:** circumstances, time, place. Striking or beating.

The triangle in the middle of the diagram above is part three of the Rereketanga model; it is my newly developed supervision framework.

Ahurutanga is found in the negotiation of the supervision process, which we have been taught is a crucial part of safe and best practice.

KO AU is us: we come with a lens that we look through, and how we see the world. **KO AU** is focused on the self, what we want in life, and ambition, but it is my view that to be effective is a negotiation.

KO KOE is the person or Whanau you Tautoko (support). They lead the plan. This is Tinorangatiratanga. The only time they don't lead the plan is if they become a danger to themselves or others.

So what is **KO IA**? This is "The Others", the unforeseen circumstances, the other agencies involved, the school, , the police, CYFS, WINZ - things or people that we have no control over. The negotiation between **KO AU**, (me) **KO KOE**, (Client/Whanau) and **KO IA** (The Others) is what creates pressure, but it is the placement of these tensions or "effective outcomes" which is discussed.

Taukumekume: It's a struggle for, to pull against each other, argue, **TA:** colour, DNA, **U:** confirmation, established, on task, **KU:** journey with no boundaries, no hindrances, **ME:** breaking things down, **Kumekume:** to pull or drag.

This model was developed in year one of my degree where we were asked to develop an assessment tool based on others.

I merged Mason Durie's writings on Te Whare Tapa Wha with western clinical "time lining", Peta Ruha "Te Pounamu", and recommendations from a lecturer (Kirsty Maxwell, 2008).

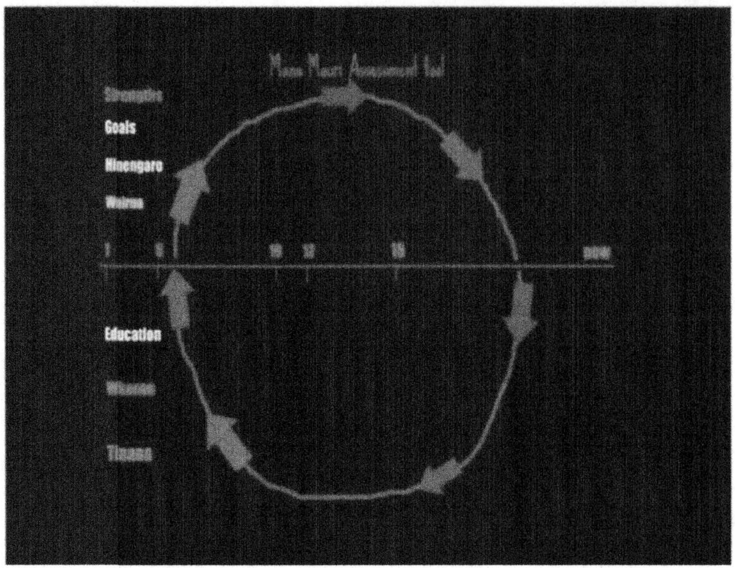

Mana Mauri initial assessment tool.

If every person (Tangata) is born into this world with a life force of unblemished decent, the object of the assessment is about whakapapa, or origins, broken down into five categories: Taha **Whanau**, Taha **Wairua**, Taha **Hinengaro**, Taha **Tinana** (Dr Mason Durie, 1982), and **education**. These are "Topics of discussion", looking at their life from birth until present.

To analyse where corresponding breakdown occurred then to look at coming up with a plan of goals based on their individual strengths. As a Youth Worker currently working for a Maori Kaupapa service, I believe that Tikanga in applied practice is important. Mana Mauri incorporates western clinical practice alongside Te Ao Maori ways of life.

"Tikanga was constructed over centuries of practice and was underpinned by core values and principles which governed Māori political, legal, social and spiritual behavior. It was flexible, adaptable and could be interconnected to fit with the demands of the moment or as new circumstances arose."
(Gallagher, 2014)

*"Tikanga originates from the two words **Tika** and **Nga** 'Tika' can be defined as right, correct, just or fair. 'Nga' is the plural for the English word 'the'. Therefore, in this context Tikanga may be defined as 'way(s) of doing and thinking held by Māori to be just and correct."*
(NZ Law Commission, 2003)

What is Mana and Mauri?

"I have Vested Authority from the Divine Source, the Ancestors. I celebrate my absolute uniqueness... there has never been anyone else exactly like me, and there never will be. I have been given Divine Authority to stand in my own power and wisdom."
(Pere, 1997)

Mauri: what is it? **MA**: pure or unblemished, **Uri**: descent.

Mamae (hurt) of dependence: the findings of research left unanswered questions.

If women are sacred, Tapu, mothers to nurture their own and take care of children that are not, why are they targeted?

Why are they treated poorly? The Ahurutanga is found with our mothers; shouldn't the way we treat them be important?

Try to reposition oneself to a "solutions-based lens", coming to the Rereketanga framework hypothesis that:

> *"We are all unique in our DNA make up and therefore require treatment based on the needs and journey defined by the individual inclusive of their Whanau."*

The model "Rereketanga" is made up of the "Mana Mauri initial assessment tool".

The "Kaitiake o Te Tangata" (triangle supervision model), which through the negotiation or placement of negative and positive tensions (Taukumekume) creates Ahurutanga.

To keep this process safe, I have had Korero with Kaumatua, Kuia, and those learned in the Reo.

To define, articulate and analyse breakdown of Maori words, with consideration of Rangahau Tikanga.

KO TE REO KIA TIKA. KO TE REO KIA RERE. KO TE REO KIA MAORI.

Chapter nine: "Aftermath"

Meetings about meetings

A few years back, I attempted to get involved with social work networks at various levels and a lot of experienced practitioners from social services, but after a while I began to observe a common theme.

Lots of discussions but little outcomes. Talk but not much doing.

Meetings about meetings.

"Working closer together" or "it's about networking".

I just could not stand to be there any longer. I love being around visionary thinkers, who are creative, that think outside the square to devise innovative concepts, but who also put them into action. I call it being a "fire starter"; you put ideas out there, and people get excited and do it.

I would much rather be with young people, encouraging them, than in a meeting about planning the next meeting.

Youth workers that don't understand youth issues should not work with young people.

I have been at clinical meetings with well-meaning and well-intentioned people that even I feel like telling to piss off. Poverty, depression, suicidal ideation, domestic violence, and crime are issues that need to be addressed, and some of the responses or lack thereof is disappointing.

Pinocchio syndrome

Years ago, I was asked to present to a group of social service providers on "the state of the youth". So I decided to use the story of Pinocchio; we as "generation x" knew, but the youth are not really familiar with him, except as a character on the movie "Shrek".

Gepetto of course was the father. "The blue fairy" brought Pinocchio to life, but took off after this. Many young people only have one parent, and find the separation of parents hard.

Pinocchio chose to hang out with "the lost boys", who were smoking, skipping school, and smashing the windows of houses. This spoke to me of the young people who have created their own groups and go on "the missions".

Jiminy Cricket is the "voice inside", who reminds Pinocchio that what he is doing isn't right or good for him.

The fairground owner coerces Pinocchio and the lost boys into the fairground, where there are "no rules": eat as much candy as you want, stay up as late as you want, skip school, etc. This spoke to me about drug use and having no boundaries.

But let me ask you, what did the fairground owner want to do?

He turned Pinocchio and his friends into donkeys, chucked them into a sack on his boat, and took them out to sea to drown them. Yes, he wanted to kill them.

Are our young people dying because they have no rules?

No boundaries?

Or is it absentee fatherism? No positive role models?

Spiritual realms

In western clinical thinking, I am unsure if mindfulness towards the concepts of Tapu or Wairuatanga or the spiritual realm are ever considered, except maybe in cultural competencies tokenised during an audit process.

When you work in mental health, there are situations that one may not be able to explain.

I have always used karakia (prayer) when in my car going to a house, and, if the situation was dangerous, when leaving too.

I believe that when bad situations or breaches of Tapu occur with individuals, family, buildings, or other areas, karakia is important, especially when going into unsafe spaces is a daily situation.
I have always had a belief that God has always had his hand of protection on my life, when many times I could have died.

I will always honour him, and his existence.

A I O

Wairua.

Urban whakapapa

Young people are often disconnected from their whakapapa but have formed an interconnectedness to their peers. In a group exercise, youth were asked to name the whakapapa of "the Simpsons". Most knew this - Bart, Lisa, Marge the mum, Homer the dad - but when it came to Iwi, Hapu, land, or waka, only a minority knew this.

Ko Tonsberg Te Maunga.
Ko Fyris Te Awa.
Ko Osberg Te Waka.
Ko Finland Te Iwi.
Ko Yngling Te Hapu.
Ko Te Viking Oku Tupuna.
Ko Yahu, Toku ingoa.

My journey to find pepeha took over three years. I encourage young people to reconnect with their culture, because if they don't, their culture will be a gang culture, a violence culture, a drug culture, a crime culture.

Remember: this is just an opinion, a view or a lens. My worldview is informed by my lived experiences, through learning Tikanga as a non-Maori. It has helped me to reconnect with my own.

War of the mind

Young people are in a war, a battle to decide what is good, or what isn't. Often we use experimentation as an excuse, but the reality is that our children are placing themselves and others at risk, because often the parental figures have failed to keep them safe.

I am often called to crisis situations where children want to die. They have nothing to live for, no purpose or hope. They are just surviving, and your thoughts become feelings, which turn into actions.

Relationship break-ups, especially with males, seem to trigger depression, which turns them to drugs or alcohol to escape from reality.

The positive thoughts alongside the negative create confusion, where compulsive decisions prove deadly.

I call it "the place of no return", where drug overdose leads to madness or death.

I remember a research paper that was done about a year ago with school students; seven out of ten admitted to experiencing suicidal thoughts. That is quite scary.

Another group were given options of connections to services. The choices were:

Social media (like Facebook), an 0800 number, or services meeting with them at school.

To my surprise, they wanted face-to-face contact. Interesting that in this technology age, they just wanted personal time; not to go to an office and be "assessed", but to actually meet and talk with a real person.

I have facilitated group programmes in schools all around Wellington for over seven years; we discuss open and honest topics such as drug use, negative relationships, problems with teachers, suicide, mental illness, CYFS, crime, and how to overcome bullying.

I remember once, during an exercise, the group was asked:

"When you were young, what did you want to be when you grew up?"

Answers included fireman, police, teacher, nurse, until one girl said:

"I wanted to be dead."

And she burst into tears.

I remember also how one critical poor decision could change a young person forever. There once was a young man who was in lock up.

The plan was recommended to return to Rarotonga to live with family, but the department didn't want to pay the airfare.

As a consequence, he ended up prospecting for a gang instead. Tied to a chair and pushed out a two story window, and he lived.

Never the same, he became homeless on the streets of Auckland, damaged for life, an alcoholic drug addict.

All it would have taken was one flight, to save him from himself.

Some of the most effective youth workers have criminal history. I believe that people with a colourful past should be allowed to support young people. The guy that mentored me was ruthless back in the day, but his life experience helped me to change my mindset. I would never have become a social worker, found employment, or got my education without that change in my mindset, from criminal to a life of purpose and hope.

I am not an expert; this book has tragic stories of youth who will never get to tell anyone about their tragic lives because they are either dead, mentally gone, or currently in wards or prison.
My friend once told me that, as a young person, he was beaten and forced to run around a field in the rain, in women's clothing. He got put in a youth lock up. One night at dinner, another youth was boasting:

"I don't care - I treat my family like shit!"

My friend picked up a fork and stabbed him in the face.

When asked why he did it, he said it was because the guy had a family who loved him.

Extreme behaviour. Extreme response.

Increased violence in society is a symptom of the underlining hurt amongst youth culture.

Conclusion

If you are currently training in social work, I'm not trying to put you off; I'm just trying to share some experiences. I was blessed to have so many senior experienced RSW, clinicians, and co-workers who mentored me. They taught me so much.

Do not get into it to make money, because you won't.

Buy hungry kids food because you care.

If you have historical problems that need counsel? Then get some. Don't think that you can fix others problems to help your own.

A wise councillor said to me once:

"We are all fucked; the more degrees we get, the better we are at hiding it."

I never became a youth worker because I was once at risk. I became a youth worker because I was told to do it. I never wanted to support youth.

You can't look after others until you can look after yourself.

Remember that young people and their families are always assessing you assessing them.

Whanau should lead and define their own journey to wellness.

Pay it forward

Once, in a place called Bondi in Australia, a young teenage boy climbed up onto the train line to jump off and commit suicide.

As he stood there, he saw a vision of himself. Wearing a suit and speaking to thousands of people. He stopped. He saw his potential.

An old lady (who happened to be driving past) stopped and helped him.

Fast-forward ten years.

That boy is grown up and pushing his three year old daughter in her pram down the street. He sees an angry young man that is homeless and offers to take him into their home. He helps him to make changes.

That angry young man was me.
If I hadn't had early intervention from a stranger and his wife who took me in, I would be dead. Or in prison.

I will always be in debt to their kindness.

Fast-forward ten years, the angry young man decides to get a job in the youth lock ups, working with the most extreme outcasts of society, the drug addicts, even the children of this country's most hated offenders and gang members.

Early intervention is the key to lasting change.

As I sat in a police cell one night with a young person, I said everything is going to be ok:

"You don't have to be like your father."

His self-worth is there, a shift.

Maybe you can change the world, one person at a time. Pay it forward, and remember the impact of your life.

True leaders and ones that love and care are needed in these dark times.

Specialists in the field need to be trained and ready.

Maori kaupapa services are needed now more than ever.

Coke on my Weet-Bix

As I sit tonight, looking down at the choice of cold baked beans and processed sausage, I reflect on an hour before when I dropped off a food parcel to a family in need (with my kids in the car), knowing that they will now have more food than us.

My mind travels to a debate I had with a well-meaning, upper class lady in a low docile school, who said:

"I don't allow my children to eat processed food."

I think about how my own family actually would be

grateful for any food right now.

How come so many children in this country are worse off than us?

Why is 2.25 litres of coke two dollars? Or why is milk around four dollars?

For many that have read this worldview on social work practice in New Zealand, it may bring feelings of sadness and concern. That's ok; maybe a reality check can be good for the soul.

A good friend of mine once said:

"Piss someone off or make them love you, but if no reaction at all, be worried."

So why am I writing this now?

This week has been a reality check for me.

As I'm typing, my daughter has shoes with holes, I have the flu, and we don't actually have enough money to survive any more. For two years now, my partner and I have had an average of one meal a day: dinner.

This is so our children have at least five items of food in their lunch boxes.

They have breakfast, lunch, and tea every day. Our lawns haven't been mowed for a month, I have a power bill five days overdue, and the bank ringing me four times a day - you get the picture.

The time is drawing near that I may leave social work, not because I want to, but because I have to put my children first. Social work will cost you, sometimes everything.

Since 2004,I have supported thousands of "at risk" young people and their families, along the way receiving a Bachelor of Social Work in Bi-culturalism, and a certificate in Mental Health, which I am so proud of. Social work cost me my first marriage (partly due to the long hours).

I will always remember what was said to me the day I decided to leave my job as a successful manager of a business to work with young people.

"You won't last in there - they will eat you up."

It has taken a while to realize my family must come first, and this is why I decided the time is right to share the journey of these young people trying to survive under the conditions that the system placed them under.

A true social worker doesn't want to be one.

A true leader doesn't want to be one, but just is.

Mauri Moe, Mauri Oho, Mauri Ora.

I'm asleep, I awaken, and I seek wellness.
I want to stop seeing our young people ending up dead or in prison.

P.S

I believe that situations in New Zealand are about to get worse. This is due to the financial crisis that has been delayed until now.

As many people begin to lose their jobs, social stressors will increase domestic violence, crime, and murder.

People will become so desperate that their hearts will grow cold. That is why social work is so important.

The recent fifty percent increase in suicide attempts in young people is an early indicator of what is to come.

There are people right now living on twenty dollars

a week for food.

As the ministry of social development attempts to save millions of dollars in the welfare state, they unconsciously will reap havoc and detrimental repercussions.

Make no mistake.

New Zealand is on the verge of a crisis like nothing this country has seen for a long time.

These are the stories of young people, from different backgrounds. Names have been replaced by characters from the popular television show "The Simpsons". Facts have been changed to protect their identities.

If you are reading this and you think it's about you, it is not. It just means that you may have had similar experiences.

We all should have a reason to live, to fight for social justice.

References

Gallagher. Timoti. (2003). *Tikanga Māori Pre-1840*, Victoria University of Wellington, New Zealand.

Gallagher, Timoti. (2014). *Te Kawa a Māui*, Victoria University of Wellington, New Zealand.

Koraunui Kaimahi. Personal communications (10/10/14, 13:00 to 16:30).

Logie, Jan. (June 23, 2014). *Work and Income – stories from hidden people.* Retrieved 23/6/14 from http://blog.greens.org.nz/2014/06/23/work-and-income-stories-from-hidden-people/

Mead, Hirini Moko. (2003). *Tikanga Maori: living by Maori values.* New Zealand: Hula publishers. Wellington, New Zealand.

NZ Law Commission. (2003). *Whakapapa,* Victoria University of Wellington, New Zealand.

Palmerston North City Council. (July 9, 1999). Survey of concerns about WINZ. Retrieved 23/6/14 from http://www.wairaka.net/ubinz/IR/1999WINZconcerns.html

Parker, H. Personal communications (30/9/14, 12:30 to 13:30) ARO, KA, Whakakaa.

Pere, Rangimarie Turuke. (1997). *Tehei*

Mauri Ora. MANU AO Academy. Retrieved 11/10/14 from http://www.manu-ao.ac.nz/massey/fms/manu-ao/documents/09-08-10%20RPere.pdf

Pere, Rangimarie Turuke. (1997). *Te Wheke, A celebration of infinite wisdom,* Page 32.
Pohatu, Taina Whakaatere. (2010). *Mauri-rethinking, Human being*, MAI Review. 2011, Vol. 3, p1-12.

Rotorua Peoples Advocacy Centre. (August 4, 2008). *Are Work And Income Breaking The Law?* Retrieved from http://info.scoop.co.nz/Rotorua_Peoples_Advocacy_Centre

Ruha, P. (1999). *Te Pounamu Model.* Workshop held at Specialist Māori Mental Health, Te Whare Marie, and Porirua Hospital Campus: Wellington.

Springford, Vomle. (Oct 9, 2013). *Wairarapa families going hungry.* Retrieved 11/10/14 from http://www.nzherald.co.nz/wairarapa-timesage/news/article.cfm?c_id=1503414&objectid=11137229

St John, Susan. (2012). *Achilles heel of National's welfare reform.* Retrieved March 2 from http://www.nzherald.co.nz/nz/news/article.cfm?c_id=1&objectid=10789075

The Beehive. (2014). *Welfare Reform Factsheet and Q & A.* Retrieved 11/10/14 from

http://www.beehive.govt.nz/sites/all/files/Welfare_F
actsheet_and_Q&A.pdf

The Maori dictionary online. (2014). Rereke,
New Zealand. Retrieved 11/10/14 from
http://www.maoridictionary.co.nz/search?idiom=&p
hrase=&proverb=&loan=&keywords=rereke&searc
h=

Trevett, Claire. (June 21, 2011). *Bennett:
Welfare reform is 'scary'.* Retrieved from
https://www.google.co.nz/webhp?sourceid=chrome
-instant&ion=1&espv=2&ie=UTF-
8#q=Claire+Trevett,+(Tuesday+June+21,+2011).+
Bennett:+Welfare+reform+is+'scary'.&spell=1

Wi Repa, Parae. Personal communications
(25/8/14, 09:00 to 11:00, and 26/9/14, 11:00 to
12:00).

WRITEHANDEDGIRL, (13/2/2014). *Terror
and humiliation – just another day with WINZ.*
Retrieved from
http://writehanded.wordpress.com/2014/03/13/fuck
-winz-yes-i-said-it/

About the Author

Yahu is a retired Youth Worker, from Aotearoa. Since 2004, Yahu supported some of the most acute cases of young people labelled as "At Risk" with mental health, disability, gangs and alcohol or drug issues.

His debut book aptly named "Dead or in Prison" tells the true story of youth in New Zealand, involved in gangs, drugs, crime and disengaged from education.

Yahu challenges the reader by opening the door into a world that many have been unaware of until now, a place of poverty, neglect and lock up.

He has worked in forensics, prison, mental health wards, schools and the community.

Yahu is an activist, father of four, musician, and public speaker, who uses hiphop culture to engage young people.

To order the book, or further enquiry email Yahu direct at; deadorinprisonbook@gmail.com

Special Thanks

To the Writers Plot Readers Read Bookshop in Upper Hutt for believing in this project by taking on my manuscript.

Writer's Plot
Readers Read

Bookshop
2 / 893 Fergusson Drive
Upper Hutt
Opposite the Upper Hutt Railway station
Business Hours
Mon – Fri 9am to 5.30pm
Saturday 10am to 2pm
Sunday closed
Phone : 04 528 4549
We stock only NZ or NZ based authors.

Email:writersplotreadersread@outlook.com
Website:www.writersplotreadersread.nz

This book is © exclusively to
http://5thfloorconsultant.blogspot.co.nz/ 2015